HUSTLERS HACKBOOK

The Ultimate Masterclass on Navigating the Hustleverse.

Chiemerie Sam Jonah

Copyright © 20124 Chiemerie Sam Jonah

All rights reserved.

ISBN: 9798325717932

DEDICATION

I dedicate this book to the memory of my late Dad. His business and career life weren't just a source of inspiration; they were a masterclass in itself, teaching me lessons far beyond what any business school could offer.

CONTENTS

	Why This Book?	i
	Acknowledgments	iv
1	Introduction	v
2	Find Your "It" Factor	Pg 1
3	Resilience Under Fire	Pg 6
4	Ruthless Time Domination	Pg 11
5	Taking Smart Gambles For Big Wins	Pg 16
6	The Weapon Of Perception	Pg 16
7	Hustle Blitz	Pg 25
8	The Art Of The Deal	Pg 30
9	The Money Game	Pg 35
10	Brothers In Arms	Pg 40
11	The Art Of War	Pg 45
12	Respect The Hustle Code	Pg 51
13	Beyond The Money	Pg 56
14	The Ever-Evolving Hustle	Pg 61
15	Conclusion: The Eternal Hustler	Pg 67
	About the Author	Pg 70

WHY THIS BOOK?

Failure, struggle, the unwavering will to keep going – that's the journey that led me here. My first business venture, importing and distributing satellite systems, crashed and I was drowning in debt, the once-promising entrepreneurial future felt like a distant memory. Even those I thought were close friends disappeared when I needed them most.

With my dreams in tatters, I reluctantly took a job sponsored by the Federal Government of Nigeria training young people in the Niger Delta on entrepreneurship. What began as a job to pay the bills soon transformed into an unexpected opportunity. My dedication and vision propelled me to a leadership position as the project manager, and in the process, I began to dissect the wounds of my past failure.

The job became a turning point. I resolved to embrace entrepreneurship once more, vowing to fight through no matter the adversity. "It's either I succeed or I succeed" became my mantra. I transitioned from a project manager to an entrepreneur offering project management services, and my relentless pursuit of excellence paid off. My reputation soared, leading to unsolicited recommendations and a string of government-sponsored projects.

In the midst of these endeavors, an idea struck me with sudden clarity – our constant struggle with logistical inefficiency. This led to creation of Obarn Trading and Logistics, a company that quickly established itself by managing logistics not only for my projects but for others as well.

As a future-oriented project management expert passionate about projects with social and economic value, I saw an opportunity to integrate technology into these initiatives. This led to Induvas Tech-Knowledge Services, a company that has grown into a group with a presence in education, real estate, healthcare, energy, hospitality, and consulting services.

Hustlers Hackbook: A Masterclass on Navigating the Hustleverse

So, who am I to write this book? I'm a hustler. I'm a fighter. I'm a survivor. But most importantly, I'm someone who failed, learned, and came back stronger. I'm living proof that you can overcome setbacks and achieve your dreams.

Let me be upfront: I may not be a literary genius, but I'm passionate about your success. This book is my battle cry, a way to join you on your thrilling journey to the top. I've turned the lessons I learned into courses designed to empower and inspire you, and those very courses form the core content of this book.

It captures the countless hours of research, the sweat of failures, and the triumphs that shaped my own path. It's a collection of insights, strategies, and hard-won wisdom from the battlefield of hustling. These pages compile some of the training notes I used for my masterclasses.

You see, my fellow hustler, the world rewards the bold, the resilient, and the adaptable. It celebrates those who dream big and take even bigger action. In these lessons, I'll share principles and practices that can turn your dreams into reality.

But remember, the power to unlock your potential lies within you. This book is just a guiding star in the vast universe of your possibilities. The real journey begins when you close these pages and take that first step toward your aspirations.

I don't know where you are right now, but I know exactly where you can be. And together, we'll journey there. As you embark on this voyage through the following words, know this: you are not alone. You have a companion in me, and the untapped potential within yourself.

Are you ready to rise and embrace the hustle? The stage is set. The world awaits your extraordinary story. Embrace the challenges, seize the opportunities, and let this book be your compass as you navigate the competitive arena of hustling. With determination, resilience, and unwavering commitment, you will not only survive but thrive. So, let's

Hustlers Hackbook: A Masterclass on Navigating the Hustleverse

turn the page and begin this transformative journey together. The world is waiting for the greatness that resides within you, and I'm here to help you unleash it.

Embrace the hustle, defy the odds, and become the force you're meant to be.

ACKNOWLEDGMENTS

I owe a huge debt of gratitude to everyone who has contributed to my success so far. There are simply too many of you to mention here, but you know who you are. There are also those whose hustle inspires me every day, and you are the reason I'm always fired up to push myself further. Thank you!

INTRODUCTION

Welcome, fellow hustlers, to this masterclass where we'll decode the secrets of navigating the hustled world- Hustleverse. On this exciting journey, I'll be your guide, sharing the wisdom I've gained as a seasoned hustler.

The word "hustle" evokes a powerful image: drive, ambition, and unwavering determination. It's more than just a trendy term; it's a way of life for successful individuals who dare to dream big and chase their goals relentlessly. Hustling is about hard work, pushing your limits, seizing opportunities, and refusing to settle for mediocrity.

Forget the fairytales. The hustle is a demanding journey, not a walk in the park. Success stories aren't handed out like participation trophies. This isn't about dusty self-help books or overpriced workshops that promise instant wealth. This book is your weapon – a masterclass for warriors, a strategic plan for those hungry enough to claim their place in the competitive world of hustle. It's your baptism by hustle, a deep dive into the heart and mind of a winner. Because in this game, you're not just playing to survive – you're here to conquer.

Let's face it: the hustle isn't for the faint of heart. It's a battlefield where only the resourceful, cunning, and determined thrive. As Mark Cuban wisely said, you must work with the relentless drive of someone who wants to take everything you've built. Fairytales of overnight success are just illusions here, and self-help books often offer little more than empty promises.

Within these pages, you'll become a master architect of your own hustle empire. We'll crack the code on navigating complex challenges, deploy battle-tested hacks, and strategize like a seasoned general. We'll dissect the psyche of true hustlers and develop the sharp mentality that separates victors from the defeated.

Hustlers Hackbook: A Masterclass on Navigating the Hustleverse

Here's the unfiltered truth: the world owes you nothing. Opportunity is a right you have to fight for, tooth and nail. This is the hustler's code – a relentless pursuit of victory with no room for consolation prizes. This arena has only one reward: domination.

Losers whine about "next time." Hustlers roar, "There's no next time, only this one, and I'm taking it all!" It's a fire in your gut, an insatiable hunger that burns brighter than the rest.

But let's be clear: the road to success is demanding. It demands blood, sweat, and tears. While your competitors sleep, you'll be burning the midnight oil, crafting strategies that will leave them in the dust. There will be moments of doubt and towering obstacles, but it's within these crucibles that champions are forged.

For those who endure, who can weather the storm and ride the raging waves, the rewards are immeasurable. Imagine outperforming your competition, ruling your niche, and etching your name in the hustler's hall of fame. The path to legendary status is paved with trials, but the glory at the end is unparalleled.

This book is your guide to becoming that legend by;

Unearthing Your Hustle Niche: Find Your "It" Factor

The hustled world is a vast arena, brimming with countless opportunities. But to thrive, you need to identify your unique hustle niche - your "it" factor. This chapter equips you with the tools for self-discovery, helping you unearth the skills, passions, and talents that will fuel your hustle journey.

Building the Unbreakable Hustler Spirit: Resilience Under Fire

The hustle journey is paved with challenges and setbacks. This chapter equips you with the "Hustler Spirit," the unwavering resilience you need to bounce back from defeats and keep pushing forward.

Hustlers Hackbook: A Masterclass on Navigating the Hustleverse

Mastering Your Time: The Hustle Clock

Time is your most valuable weapon in the hustle arena. This chapter equips you with powerful productivity strategies to outwork your competition and achieve maximum output.

Mastering Calculated Risk: Taking Smart Gambles for Big Wins

Playing it safe often leads to stagnation. Calculated risks, however, can propel you towards significant gains. This chapter teaches you how to assess risks strategically and make calculated gambles that propel your hustle forward.

Building Your Hustle Brand: The Power of Perception

In a world where perception is reality, your personal brand is your ultimate weapon. This chapter delves into the art of building a powerful brand, teaching you to craft a compelling image that commands respect, positions you as a leader, and leaves your rivals in the dust.

Hustle Blitz: Launching Your Hustle Empire at Lightning Speed

The competition waits for no one. This chapter equips you with the strategies for a rapid-fire hustle launch, allowing you to dominate your market before your rivals even know what hit them.

Mastering the Hustle Arena: The Art of the Deal

The hustle arena thrives on effective communication, persuasion, and the ability to close deals. This chapter equips you with the essential tools to secure clients, win negotiations, and dominate the competition.

The Money Game: Financial Strategies for Hustle Dominance

Hustle isn't just about passion; it's about building a sustainable and profitable business. This chapter equips you with advanced financial tactics to maximize your income streams, outmaneuver competitors, and build a financial war chest to fuel your long-term success.

Forging Strategic Alliances: Brothers in Arms

Even the lone wolves need backup sometimes. This chapter delves into the art of building strategic partnerships – alliances that multiply your strength and influence.

The Art of War: Strategies for Hustle Domination

The hustle jungle operates on its own set of rules. Here, you'll learn the advanced tactics and strategies for outmaneuvering your rivals and securing dominance.

Decoding the Hustle Code: Respect the Game

The hustle jungle has its own language, ethics, and legal landscape. Understanding these elements is crucial for navigating its complexities and emerging victorious.

The Hustle Dividend: Beyond the Money

Effective hustling offers a rich harvest beyond just financial rewards. This chapter explores the diverse rewards that come from the hustle journey.

The Ever-Evolving Hustle: Staying Ahead of the Curve

The hustle landscape is constantly evolving. This chapter emphasizes the importance of continuous learning and adaptation to ensure your hustle remains relevant and dominant.

This, hustlers, is just the beginning.

Remember, the greatest hustle is the one you wage on yourself. So, are

Hustlers Hackbook: A Masterclass on Navigating the Hustleverse

you ready to embark on this epic journey? Are you prepared to push your boundaries, conquer your fears, and rewrite the rules of the game? The world of high-stakes competition awaits your arrival. Lace up your gloves, sharpen your focus, and let's dive headfirst into the fray.

FIND YOUR "IT" FACTOR

"Being a master of nothing is a recipe for failure. Find your niche, and own it." - Chiemerie Sam Jonah

Welcome, fellow hustlers! Prepare to embark on a journey into the dynamic world of opportunity – the hustle landscape. It's a vast and ever-changing terrain, brimming with potential. However, without a clear direction, you risk getting lost in its complexity. The truth is, trying to be a master of everything at once is a recipe for failure in the hustle game. That's where your unique "it" factor comes in: your distinctive hustle niche. It's the key to navigating this world with precision and achieving unparalleled success.

While general skills have their place, specialization reigns supreme in the hustle arena. It's crucial to determine what sets you apart and which platform you can leverage to your advantage. Every successful hustler began with a single focus and expanded from there. So, identify your niche and devote yourself to mastering it.

Now, let's dig deeper into the process of self-discovery, where we'll unearth the hidden treasures within you – the skills, passions, and talents that will fuel your journey in the hustle world.

How to Uncover Your Elusive "It" Factor

Hustlers Hackbook: A Masterclass on Navigating the Hustleverse

Let's break it down into three essential steps:

Exploring the Hustle Landscape

The hustle world is diverse, with each sector representing a distinct niche. From tech startups to e-commerce marketplaces, from artist studios to inventor labs – each offers unique opportunities and challenges. The key lies in finding the niche that resonates with your soul. As Gary Vaynerchuk once said, "Differentiation, not competition, is the name of the game." Take the time to explore various hustle niches, conduct research, engage with online communities, and seek advice from established hustlers. This exploration will spark ideas and help you identify areas that align with your interests.

Meet Remi, who transitioned from a quiet librarian to a sought-after information broker in the competitive world of corporate intelligence. Remi's journey began with her passion for research and her uncanny ability to find information that others couldn't. By recognizing these unique skills as her "it" factor, she carved a niche that combined her love for libraries with the cutthroat demand of information brokerage.

The quote by Albert Einstein perfectly captures the essence of finding your hustle niche: "The person who follows the crowd will usually go no further than the crowd. The person who walks alone is likely to find themselves in places no one has ever been before." It's about not just going where the path may lead, but creating your own path and leaving a trail.

The Hustler Audit: Identifying Your Interests

The Hustler Audit is a rigorous self-assessment that lays bare your strengths and weaknesses, akin to a public financial audit. But fear not, for knowledge is power. By recognizing your blind spots and amplifying your strengths, you'll craft a hustle strategy that outshines the competition.

Hustlers Hackbook: A Masterclass on Navigating the Hustleverse

Let's get personal. The ultimate weapon of any hustler isn't fancy technology or a hefty marketing budget – it's you. We need to dissect what makes you **YOU**. Your blend of skills, passions, and experiences sets you apart. As entrepreneur Gary Vaynerchuk advises, "Find your sweet spot, where passion meets skill." What are you naturally talented at? What fuels your passion?

Meet Funmi, a practice manager at a bustling law firm who turned her love for baking into a thriving online cake business. Even though she manages legal practitioners by day and unleashes her passion at night, she started small, selling cupcakes at the office. Her unique flavor combinations and artistic flair set her apart. Funmi identified her strengths (baking) and interests (creativity) and found a niche in the crowded dessert market. Her passion for baking, combined with her natural artistic talent, became her booming hustle.

Maybe you're a whiz with social media, but spreadsheets make you yawn. There's a thriving niche for social media management, where you can help businesses build their online presence.

Here's how to conduct your hustler audit:

- Make a list of your top skills and interests.
- Research different hustle niches that align with your strengths.
- Brainstorm how you can combine your skills and interests into a unique niche.
- Is there a market for it? What are the existing players? How can you stand out?
- **The Venn Diagram of Opportunity:** Draw three overlapping circles: one for what you love (passions), one for what you are skilled at (talents), and one for potential market needs (opportunities). The sweet spot, where all three circles intersect, is your potential hustle niche.

Discover Your Competitive Edge

Hustlers Hackbook: A Masterclass on Navigating the Hustleverse

Now that you've identified your niche — that sweet spot where your skills and passions collide — it's time to uncover your competitive edge. The hustle world is a crowded space, just like a Black Friday sale. To rise above the noise, you need a sharp weapon — a deep understanding of your competitive edge.

Remember David and Goliath? Sure, Goliath was a hulking giant, but David had one crucial advantage — his agility. He used his strength (mobility) to exploit Goliath's weakness (size) and emerged victorious. You, the hustler David, need to identify your agility — what sets you apart from the Goliaths in your niche?

Hustle legend Gary Vaynerchuk says, "You don't need to be the best; you just need to be different." Find your unique voice, shout it from the rooftops, and watch the world take notice.

Armed with a clear understanding of your strengths, interests, and competitive edge, the next step is to validate and refine your findings.

Micro-Testing Your Niche

Before fully committing to a niche, test it out. Start small by offering a minimal viable product (MVP) or simplified service. Gather feedback and iterate. This iterative process not only hones your niche but also builds confidence and expertise.

Take inspiration from the culinary world's pop-up concept, where chefs test new ideas with temporary restaurants. Similarly, launch a temporary online store, offer a short course, or host a one-time event. This approach gauges interest and provides valuable insights into market demand and operational challenges.

The world awaits your unique brand of hustle.

There's no shame in starting small and narrowing down your niche as you progress. Unearthing your hustle niche isn't about conforming to

Hustlers Hackbook: A Masterclass on Navigating the Hustleverse

predefined categories but creating a space uniquely yours. Remember, the hustle world rewards the bold, the innovative, and those unafraid to forge new paths. Find your "it" factor, and success will follow.

Your niche serves as your launchpad, the foundation upon which you'll build your hustle empire. So, take your time, explore, and don't hesitate to experiment. Once you uncover your "it" factor, the hustle world will bow to your prowess. The world awaits your unique brand of hustle.

In our upcoming masterclass, we'll delve into the "Hustler Spirit," exploring how to cultivate the resilience needed to overcome setbacks and emerge stronger in the hustle arena. Until then, Let's get hustling!

RESILIENCE UNDER FIRE

"Success is not final, failure is not fatal: It is the courage to continue that counts."
— *Winston Churchill*

Alright, hustlers, welcome back to the grind! We've carved out your niche. Now, get ready for the real test – the hustle battlefield. There will be roadblocks, detours, and moments where you'll question your sanity. But fear not, because the true mark of a champion isn't the absence of struggle; it's the unwavering Hustler Spirit – the resilience that allows you to dust yourself off, learn from your mistakes, and keep pushing forward. It's the spirit that separates the pretenders from the contenders, the quitters from the hustlers who conquer.

Building the Unbreakable Hustler Spirit

Let's build the mental toughness, the grit and tenacity you need to weather any storm, forge nerves of steel, and master the art of the comeback. This is what makes an unbreakable hustler, someone who laughs in the face of setbacks and emerges stronger after every defeat. Remember, the hustle journey is a marathon, not a sprint. You need the stamina of a champion to go the distance.

Developing Grit & Tenacity

The hustle journey ain't a walk in the park. There will be days when rejections pile up like dirty laundry, and self-doubt whispers sweet nothings in your ear. That's when you need grit – the unwavering determination to push through, even when it feels impossible.

Picture marathon runners facing a steep incline. With each step, their muscles ache, their lungs burn, but their determination never wavers. Remember this: there will be days when motivation wanes and shiny object syndrome beckons. But developing grit and tenacity – the unwavering determination to see things through, no matter how long it takes – is paramount to overcoming obstacles and persevering through tough times.

Think of it like this: building a successful hustle is like sculpting a masterpiece. There will be chipping away, refining, and moments where you just want to chuck the whole thing in the trash. But with grit, you chip away day by day, transforming a rough block of stone into a work of art.

Remember J.K. Rowling, the author of the Harry Potter series? Her manuscript was rejected by 12 publishers before becoming a global phenomenon. Grit kept her going, and look where it got her – the richest author alive!

Meet James, a young entrepreneur whose startup faced financial ruin in its infancy. Despite the mounting pressure and naysayers predicting his demise, James refused to succumb to defeat. Through sheer grit and determination, he pivoted his business model, secured new investors, and ultimately transformed his company into a thriving success.

Success is not defined by the absence of failure but by the courage to persevere despite it. These words resonate deeply in the hustle world.

Here's how to cultivate grit:

- Set SMART goals: Specific, Measurable, Achievable, Relevant, and Time-bound goals give you a clear path and a sense of accomplishment as you tick them off.

- Celebrate small wins: Every step forward is a victory. Acknowledge your progress, no matter how small.
- Find your "why": What drives you? Connecting your hustle to a deeper purpose fuels your motivation.
- Embrace the power of community: Surround yourself with other hustlers who understand the struggle. Their support and shared experiences will keep you going.

Forging Mental Toughness

Pressure. Deadlines. Client demands. And sometimes, the competition just seems unbeatable. The hustle life can be mentally taxing. The pressure cooker of the hustle world can crack even the most resolute spirit. That's where mental toughness comes in. It's the ability to maintain focus and composure under pressure, control your emotions, and bounce back from setbacks stronger than ever.

Think of it this way: Imagine a champion boxer. He trains relentlessly, not just his body, but his mind as well. He learns to control his emotions and stay laser-focused on the fight. The opponent sometimes lands punches, but he doesn't crumble. He weathers the storm, strategizes, and comes back swinging even harder. That's mental toughness in action.

Here's how to build mental toughness:

- Practice mindfulness: Meditation and breathing exercises help you manage stress and maintain focus.
- Visualization: See yourself achieving your goals. Mental rehearsal strengthens your resolve.
- Challenge negative thoughts: Don't let self-doubt creep in. Identify negative thought patterns and replace them with empowering and positive affirmations.

The Art of the Comeback

Hustlers Hackbook: A Masterclass on Navigating the Hustleverse

Let's be honest, hustlers, setbacks are inevitable. Even the most successful hustlers face failures. But the true measure of a champion lies in their ability to bounce back. You'll face failures, rejections, and moments where you want to throw in the towel. But here's the secret – successful hustlers don't dwell on defeat. They master the art of the comeback.

Nelson Mandela once said, "Our greatest glory is not in never falling, but in rising every time we fall." Learn from your mistakes, adapt your strategies, and use those failures as stepping stones to future success.

Here's how to turn setbacks into springboards:

- Analyze the failure: What went wrong? Learn from your mistakes so you don't repeat them.
- Maintain a positive attitude: Don't let setbacks define you. See them as opportunities for growth. View failures as learning opportunities, not roadblocks.
- Use the fire within: Channel frustration and disappointment into renewed motivation.
- Seek support: Talk to a mentor, friend, or therapist. Sharing your struggles can be cathartic and help you gain perspective.

Go and prove that you have what it takes

In the hustle world, resilience is not just a trait; it's a necessity. By cultivating the Hustler Spirit — a blend of grit, tenacity, and mental toughness —, you'll transform from a fragile dreamer into a relentless hustler, capable of weathering any storm. Building the Unbreakable Hustler Spirit is a lifelong pursuit. But with the right tools, you can transform yourself into a hustler who thrives under pressure. Remember, champions aren't born – they're forged in the fires of adversity. Now, go out there and prove you have what it takes!

In our next masterclass, we'll explore "Ruthless Productivity Domination," where we'll delve into the art of Mastering the

Hustlers Hackbook: A Masterclass on Navigating the Hustleverse Hustle Clock, Unleashing Peak Performance, Prioritization Like a Gladiator and Building Your Hustle Engine. Until then, keep pushing forward, stay resilient, and let your Hustler Spirit soar.

RUTHLESS TIME DOMINATION

"Time is what we want most, but what we use worst." — *William Penn*

Alright, hustlers! Buckle up, because we're about to enter the thunderdome of productivity – time management. Time, my friends, is the ultimate battlefield currency. You can have all the talent and grit in the world, but if you can't manage your minutes, you'll be crushed by the competition. But fear not, for I, your hustle coach, am here to equip you with the ruthless productivity strategies to squeeze every drop of potential out of your day and outwork everyone in your path.

Unleashing Peak Performance

Let's face it, there are only 24 hours in a day. The key isn't wishing for more time, it's about squeezing every ounce of potential out of the precious minutes you have. We're talking time management on steroids, productivity hacks that would make even a seasoned orchestra conductor envious. Imagine a conductor orchestrating a symphony – every movement deliberate, every note timed to perfection. Similarly, mastering time management and productivity is about orchestrating your day to unleash peak performance. Time management isn't enough. We're talking about peak performance. Time management guru Brian Tracy once said, "There's no magic in time management. It's simply a matter of planning and execution." We'll utilize time management techniques and productivity hacks to transform you into a hustling machine.

Meet Obinna, a serial entrepreneur known for his relentless work ethic

Hustlers Hackbook: A Masterclass on Navigating the Hustleverse

and laser-sharp focus. Despite juggling multiple ventures simultaneously, Obinna consistently delivered exceptional results. His secret? A meticulous approach to time management, incorporating techniques such as time blocking, the Pomodoro Method, and batching tasks to optimize efficiency and productivity.

In the hustle world, success belongs to those who master the art of utilizing time wisely.

Here's how to unleash your peak performance:

- Become a scheduling master: Craft a daily schedule that blocks out time for focused work, breaks, and personal life. Treat this schedule like the gospel – no sacred cows allowed.
- Embrace the power of "to-do" lists: Write down everything you need to accomplish, then prioritize ruthlessly. Focus on high-impact tasks that move the needle in your hustle journey.
- Master the art of saying no: Don't be afraid to politely decline requests that drain your time and energy. Remember, your time is your most valuable asset – spend it wisely.
- Tame the technology beast: Social media, email – they're productivity vampires. Schedule designated check-in times and silence notifications during focused work periods.

Prioritization Like a Gladiator

There's a saying in the hustle arena: "Not all tasks are created equal." Some tasks propel your hustle forward, while others are just time-sucking demons. Ruthless prioritization is your weapon to slay these demons and focus on what truly matters. You need to become a master strategist, identifying the high-impact tasks that deserve your laser focus and ruthlessly eliminating everything else.

Imagine you are a freelance writer. Do you spend hours agonizing over your social media presence, or do you prioritize crafting killer content that lands you high-paying clients? Focus on the tasks that generate income and propel your hustle forward.

Consider the analogy of a gladiator entering the arena. Do you think he wastes time fiddling with his sandals? No way! He focuses on the opponent, strategizes his attack, and prioritizes his survival. That's the hustler mindset – laser focus on the high-impact tasks that will deliver the biggest wins and eliminate the rest.

Here are some prioritization techniques that get things done:

- The Eisenhower Matrix: This powerful tool helps categorize tasks based on urgency and importance. Focus on urgent and important tasks first, schedule less urgent but important tasks, delegate or eliminate urgent but unimportant tasks, and ruthlessly discard unimportant and not urgent tasks.
- The Pareto Principle (the 80/20 rule): 80% of your results will come from 20% of your efforts. Identify the 20% of tasks that drive 80% of your results and prioritize those ruthlessly.
- Learn to say no: Don't be afraid to politely decline requests that don't align with your priorities. Your time is valuable, so protect it fiercely.

Building Your Hustle Engine

Even the most badass hustler can't run on fumes forever. The hustle is a marathon, not a sprint. Burning the candle at both ends is a recipe for burnout. To dominate the long game, you need to build a sustainable hustle engine. This means maintaining focus, staying motivated, and prioritizing a healthy work-life balance to avoid burnout. Remember this: Success in the hustle world is not just about working hard; it's about working smart and sustaining your momentum over the long term.

Think of it like this: A race car needs regular pit stops for fuel and maintenance. You, the hustler, are the race car. Take breaks to recharge, prioritize sleep, and don't neglect your health. A burnt-out hustler is no

Hustlers Hackbook: A Masterclass on Navigating the Hustleverse

hustler at all.

Consider the analogy of a marathon runner pacing themselves for a long race. They maintain a steady rhythm, fuel their body with nourishment, and listen to their signals to avoid burnout. Similarly, building your hustle engine requires a balance of focus, motivation, and self-care.

Here's how to fuel your hustle engine:

- Embrace the power of "no": Don't be afraid to say no to requests that drain your time and energy. Protect your focus for high-impact activities.
- Schedule breaks and self-care: Take regular breaks to avoid burnout. Exercise, meditate, spend time with loved ones – a refreshed hustler is a productive hustler.
- Delegate and outsource: Don't be a one-man show. Delegate tasks or outsource them to free up your time for core hustle activities.
- Reward yourself: Celebrate your wins, both big and small. Acknowledgement fuels motivation and keeps you pushing forward.
- Maintain a healthy lifestyle: Eat nutritious foods, exercise regularly, and prioritize sleep. A healthy body and mind are essential for hustle domination.

Unleash your peak performance and crush your goals.

By mastering the hustle clock, you become the master of your destiny and transform from a scattered hustler into a productivity powerhouse. Remember, hustlers, time waits for no one and it is your most valuable asset. So, unleash your peak performance, prioritize ruthlessly, and build a sustainable hustle engine that dominates the clock and crushes the competition. Now go out there and conquer your goals!

In the next masterclass, we'll explore "The Art of Taking Smart

Gambles," where we'll delve into the strategies and tactics for taking calculated risks. We'll discuss: Developing frameworks for analyzing potential risks and rewards, Discovering how to leverage calculated risks to stay ahead of the curve, seize opportunities, and outmaneuver your competition. Until then, keep dominating the hustle clock, and may your productivity be relentless and your results extraordinary.

TAKING SMART GAMBLES FOR BIG WINS

"The biggest risk is not taking any risk. In a world that's changing quickly, the only strategy that is guaranteed to fail is not taking risks." — Mark Zuckerberg

Alright, hustlers, welcome back to the grind! Today, we'll discuss the lifeblood of any successful hustle – calculated risk.

Playing it safe might prevent some bumps and bruises, but it guarantees mediocrity. Explosive growth often comes with taking smart gambles. The hustle world rewards the bold – those who are willing to take strategic risks. But fear not, because calculated risks aren't blind leaps of faith. They're well-measured decisions backed by analysis and a healthy dose of hustle bravado. As your hustle coach, I'll equip you with the framework that will transform you into a risk-assessment ninja, helping you identify and seize opportunities that propel your hustle forward, leaving your competition in the dust.

Risk Assessment Framework

The hustle world isn't a casino. Throwing darts in the dark and hoping for the best won't do. Before you jump off a metaphorical cliff, you need a parachute – a risk assessment framework. Calculated risks involve strategic analysis. We need a framework to assess the potential risks and rewards before taking the plunge. This framework is your personal crystal ball, helping you see potential roadblocks and opportunities before you commit.

Imagine you're presented with a juicy investment opportunity – high potential returns, but also a significant risk of failure. Instead of diving headfirst, you use your framework to assess the potential risks (market trends, market saturation, high investment costs) and rewards (high profit margins, first-mover advantage, competitor analysis). With this knowledge, you can make an informed decision: does the reward outweigh the risk? Should you pursue the opportunity?

Meet Olumide, a venture capitalist renowned for his keen eye for opportunities. Olumide's success wasn't a result of blind luck, but of meticulous risk assessment. By conducting thorough due diligence, analyzing market trends, and evaluating potential returns, he identified high-potential investments that yielded exponential gains.

In a rapidly evolving world, the refusal to take risks can be the greatest risk of all.

Here's how to build your Risk Assessment Framework:

- **Potential Benefits:** What are the best-case scenarios? How will this decision benefit your hustle? Increased revenue, market share dominance, industry recognition?
- **Potential Downsides:** What could go wrong? Financial loss, reputational damage, wasted time and resources?
- **Mitigation Strategies:** How can you minimize potential losses? If things go south, what's your backup plan? Risk management strategies, exit strategies?

Making Smart Decisions

So, you've assessed the risks and rewards. Now comes the moment of truth – making the decision. Here's the key: don't gamble blindly. Hustlers are strategic risk-takers. They weigh the potential benefits against the downsides and make calculated bets with a high chance of success.

Think of it like this: A chess grandmaster doesn't just move pieces randomly. They analyze the board, anticipate their opponent's moves, and calculate the potential outcomes before making their next move. That's the hustler mindset – strategic thinking before taking action.

Here's how to make smart decisions:

- **Don't be afraid to say no:** Not every opportunity is worth the risk. Learn to walk away from deals that don't align with your goals.
- **Consider your risk tolerance:** How much are you comfortable putting on the line?
- **Don't bet the farm:** Always have a safety net. Calculated risks shouldn't jeopardize your entire hustle.
- **Start small:** As you build your confidence, gradually increase the scale of your calculated risks.
- **Learn from experience:** Every risk, successful or not, is a valuable lesson. Analyze your decisions and adapt your risk assessment framework as needed.
- **Seek expert advice:** If the decision is complex, consult with mentors or advisors who can offer valuable insights.

Leveraging Calculated Moves

Calculated risks aren't just about avoiding disaster. They're powerful tools for hustlers who want to get ahead.

Meet Emmanuel, a startup founder who disrupted an industry by boldly entering uncharted territory. While others hesitated, fearing failure, Emmanuel recognized the potential rewards outweighed the risks. Through calculated moves and strategic gambles, Emmanuel not only outmaneuvered competitors but also established himself as a trailblazer in his field.

By taking smart gambles, you can:

- **Stay ahead of the curve:** Be the first to enter a new market, adopt a new technology, or launch a disruptive product.

Hustlers Hackbook: A Masterclass on Navigating the Hustleverse

- **Seize fleeting opportunities:** The hustle world is full of temporary openings. Calculated risks allow you to capitalize on them before they disappear.
- **Negotiate better deals:** Calculated risks can give you leverage in negotiations. You might be able to secure a lower price, better terms, or even exclusivity by demonstrating your willingness to take a calculated chance.
- **Outmaneuver your competition:** While your competitors play it safe, you can make calculated moves that leave them in the dust. Imagine your competitor hesitating over a new market opportunity, fearing potential risks. By taking a calculated gamble and entering the market first, you can establish a strong foothold and make it difficult for them to compete.

Make your gambles be calculated and your wins be monumental.

The business magnate, Elon Musk, once said, "If something is important enough, even if the odds are against you, you should still do it." Don't be afraid to take calculated risks, hustlers. Mastering calculated risk is the secret weapon of the most successful hustlers. By using the Risk Assessment Framework, making smart decisions, and leveraging calculated moves, you'll transform yourself from a risk-averse player to a strategic gambler who controls the odds and hustles your way to the top. Now, go out there and take some calculated risks – but remember, always play to win!

In the next masterclass, we'll delve into "The Weapon of Perception; Forging Your Hustle Brand," where we'll explore how to: Master the art of personal branding for the cutthroat world of hustle, Develop a compelling brand narrative that sets you apart from the competition, Learn strategies for building a loyal following who believe in you and your hustle. Until then, keep honing your risk-taking skills, and may your gambles be calculated and your wins be monumental.

THE WEAPON OF PERCEPTION

"Your brand is what people say about you when you're not in the room." — Jeff Bezos

Alright, hustlers, welcome back! We've conquered time, mastered risk, and built an unbreakable spirit. Now, let's dive into the battlefield of perception – your hustle brand.

In the hustle world, perception is not just reality; it's currency. It's the story people tell themselves about you, the image that pops into their minds when your name is mentioned. This intensive guide to brand building will transform you from a promising contender into a legendary hustler, teaching you to craft a powerful identity that screams authority, attracts dream clients, and positions you as the undisputed hustle champion. Your brand is your armor, your weapon, and your ultimate marketing tool. It's how you project yourself to the world, how you command respect, and how you leave your competition in the dust.

The Art of Hustle Warfare

In the hustled world, your brand is your weapon. It's the shield that protects your reputation and the sword that cuts through the competition. Here, the weapons are not swords and shields but words and images. Let's leverage the art of persuasion, build an unshakeable reputation, and position you as the go-to choice for anyone seeking your expertise.

Hustlers Hackbook: A Masterclass on Navigating the Hustleverse

Think of it like this: Imagine two freelance graphic designers. One has a polished online portfolio showcasing their work, glowing client testimonials, and a clear brand message. The other has a messy website and a social media presence filled with cat videos. Who do you think a potential client will trust with their brand identity?

Here's another way to understand it: Two companies sell athletic shoes. One has a generic logo and forgettable slogan. The other has a sleek brand identity, a passionate founder with a compelling story, and a reputation for quality. Who are you more likely to buy from? That's the power of a well-crafted brand.

Your brand is not just a logo or a tagline; it's the collective impression people have of you. In the hustle world, shaping that perception is paramount.

Here's your Brand Warfare Arsenal:

- **Define your brand pillars:** Clarity is king. What are your core values? What makes you different from the competition? These pillars form the foundation of your brand identity.
- **Craft your narrative:** Content is your chariot. Develop a compelling story that showcases your expertise, experience, and the unique value you offer clients.
- **Social media savvy:** Master the art of storytelling on social media platforms. Engage with your audience, build relationships, and establish yourself as a thought leader. Use your brand narrative to capture attention, build trust, and inspire action.

Crafting Your Champion Persona

Your brand is more than just a name; it's a story — your story. You need to develop a compelling champion persona that resonates with your target audience. Your brand isn't just a logo or a tagline; it's a compelling narrative. This narrative showcases your expertise, experience, and the unique value you offer. It's not just about

Hustlers Hackbook: A Masterclass on Navigating the Hustleverse

showcasing your skills; it's about revealing the person behind the hustle. It's the story that separates you from the pack and positions you as the champion your clients need. Gary Vaynerchuk, the social media guru, once said, "Your personal brand is a billboard. Make sure it's sending the right message to the right people."

Think of it like this, Muhammad Ali wasn't just a boxer; he was a brand. His charisma, confidence, and trash-talking all contributed to his legendary persona, making him even more formidable in the ring.

Remember Funmi, the practice manager who turned baking into a business? Her brand narrative wasn't just about cupcakes; it was about creating delicious treats with unexpected flavor combinations and a focus on locally sourced ingredients. This story resonated with customers, making her stand out in the crowded bakery scene.

Here's how to craft your brand persona:

- **Identify your ideal client:** Who are you trying to reach? Understanding their needs and values is crucial for crafting a persona that resonates.
- **Develop your brand voice:** How do you want to be perceived? Professional? Approachable? Funny? Ensure your voice shines through in all your communication. Establish a consistent voice that reflects your personality and resonates with your audience. Tell your audience who you are, what you do, and why you do it.
- **Invest in your visuals:** High-quality visuals, from your logo to your website design, create a professional first impression and elevate your brand.
- **Cultivate your online presence:** Your website and social media platforms are your digital storefront. Ensure they are polished, professional, and reflective of your brand identity.
- **Share your hustle journey:** People connect with authenticity. Share your struggles, your successes, and the lessons learned along the way. Your journey will inspire and motivate your audience.

- **Be authentic and consistent:** Don't try to be someone you're not. Authenticity builds trust and loyalty. However, maintain consistency in your messaging and brand image across all platforms.

From Gladiator to Legend

In the hustle world, building a brand is not just about attracting clients; it's about building a tribe — a loyal following that rallies behind your cause. These are your loyal supporters, your raving fans, the people who will champion your hustle to the world. A true champion doesn't fight alone. We need to build a loyal following, a community of supporters who believe in you and your hustle. Gary Vaynerchuk, the social media guru, famously said, "Jab, Jab, Jab, Right Hook." Provide valuable content consistently (jabs) before the occasional promotional message (right hook). This fosters trust and cultivates a loyal community around your brand. Think of Elon Musk. He doesn't just sell electric cars and rockets; he sells a vision — a future of sustainable transportation and space exploration. His passionate brand storytelling has built a legion of loyal fans, turning him from a tech entrepreneur into a modern-day legend.

Meet Jibola, a fitness coach who built a thriving community around his brand. Through social media engagement, live events, and exclusive content, Jibola fostered a sense of belonging among his followers. They weren't just customers; they were disciples, evangelizing his brand to the world.

Here's how to grow your following:

- **Be active on social media:** But don't just broadcast; engage! Respond to comments, answer questions, and participate in online conversations. Show people you care about them and build relationships.
- **Offer valuable content:** Share your expertise, insights, and experiences through blog posts, social media content, or even free

webinars – anything that provides your audience with valuable insights or entertainment. People follow those who provide value.
- **Build partnerships:** Collaborate with other hustlers in complementary niches. This expands your reach and exposes your brand to a new audience.

keep forging your brand, and may your perception be as formidable as your hustle.

In the hustle world, your brand is your most valuable asset. By forging a powerful hustle brand, you become more than just a hustler; you become a legend in the making. You command respect, attract the best clients, and leave the competition in your wake. Remember, perception is power — so craft your brand with intention, tell your story with conviction, build a community of loyal fans, and let your hustle brand become your greatest ally. The world awaits your legendary brand!

In our next masterclass, we'll explore "Hustle Blitz," where we'll delve into the strategies and tactics for Launching Your Hustle Empire, transforming your hustle idea into a viable and scalable empire. Until then, keep forging your brand, and may your perception be as formidable as your hustle.

HUSTLE BLITZ

"The way to get started is to quit talking and begin doing." — Walt Disney

Alright, hustlers! Buckle up tight because we're about to hit the gas on your hustle journey! The competition is fierce, and hesitation is the enemy. This is your guide to the Hustle Blitz, a lightning-fast launch strategy that gets your hustle empire off the ground before your rivals even know what hit them.

Remember, in the hustled world, speed is king. The first-mover advantage is real. While your rivals are bogged down in planning and overthinking it, you'll be out there dominating your market. Get ready to propel your glimmer idea to a full-fledged hustle empire in record time.

From Idea to Empire

Every empire begins with a brilliant hustle idea – a spark of inspiration that has the potential to ignite a revolution, be it a product, a service, a game-changing solution. But how do you transform that idea into a viable and scalable business model? Don't overthink it and get stuck in the planning phase. We're not building spaceships here; we're launching hustles! Don't let your hustle dream languish in the land of "what ifs."

Think of it like this: Richard Branson didn't spend years researching the airline industry before launching Virgin Atlantic. He saw a gap in the market, acted fast, and disrupted the entire industry. You, too, can identify a need, develop a solution, and launch your hustle with lightning speed.

Meet Steve, a visionary entrepreneur who revolutionized the tech industry with the launch of his startup. Steve's journey began with a simple idea scribbled on a napkin – a vision of a world where technology empowered individuals and transformed industries. Through strategic planning, relentless execution, and unwavering determination, Steve turned that idea into a global empire, forever changing the landscape of business.

In the hustle world, action is everything. Ideas alone are meaningless without execution.

Here's your Idea Launch Toolbox:

- Rapid idea validation: Don't waste time on elaborate business plans. Test your idea with potential customers, gather feedback, and iterate quickly.
- The Lean Startup Approach: Focus on building a Minimum Viable Product (MVP) – a basic version of your offering – and get it in front of your target audience. Their feedback will guide you in refining and iterating your product or service for maximum impact.
- Embrace the lean startup methodology: Focus on building, measuring, and learning. Continuously adapt your product or service based on customer feedback and market trends.
- The power of bootstrapping: You don't need millions in funding to launch. Bootstrap your hustle with your own resources, pre-sales, or creative financing options.

Building Your Hustle War Machine

Launching a hustle isn't just about the idea; it's about the execution. Now we need to build the hustle war machine – the infrastructure that gets your product or service into the hands of your customers, a well-oiled system that gets your business up and running in record time.

Hustlers Hackbook: A Masterclass on Navigating the Hustleverse

Michael Jordan? He didn't win championships by himself. He needed a strong supporting team – coaches, trainers, and skilled teammates. Your hustle war machine is your team – the legal and financial structures, marketing strategies, and operational systems that support your growth.

Remember Funmi, the practice manager who turned her passion for baking into a booming online cake business? She didn't wait for a million-dollar investment. She researched and registered her home-based business, obtained the necessary licenses, and started small, selling at offices and taking custom orders.

Here's your Hustle War Machine Toolbox:

- Understand your legal requirements: Research and comply with all legal and regulatory requirements for your specific hustle and location.
- Bootstrap or Bust: You don't need a mountain of cash to launch. Explore bootstrapping techniques, creative financing options, or even crowdfunding to get your hustle off the ground.
- Embrace technology: Leverage online tools and platforms to build your website, manage your finances, and automate tasks. Technology is your friend; use it to streamline your operations and free up your time to hustle.
- Building your team: Identify the skills and expertise you need, outsource tasks, hire freelancers, or assemble a team of hustlers who share your vision and can help you scale.

Scaling for Domination

Hustle Blitzes aren't about one-hit wonders. We're talking about laying the foundation for a thriving hustle empire. Here's where we develop strategies for rapid growth, building efficient systems, and scaling your operations to handle increasing demand. Do you think Jeff Bezos started Amazon with the goal of selling just a few books? He had a vision for world domination (well, almost), and he scaled his business strategically to achieve it. You too, can build a scalable hustle model poised for explosive growth. Mark Zuckerberg didn't build Facebook into a social media giant overnight. He built scalable systems and processes that allowed the platform to accommodate millions of users. You need the same foresight to ensure your hustle can weather explosive growth.

Here's how to scale your Hustle:

- **Automate, automate, automate:** Identify repetitive tasks and automate them with technology. This frees up your time to focus on higher-level activities like strategy and growth.
- **Build a winning team:** As you scale, consider building a team of talented individuals who complement your skillset. Delegate tasks, empower your team, and watch your hustle empire flourish.
- **Develop efficient workflows:** Streamline your operations to ensure smooth execution of core business functions.
- **Build a sales and marketing machine:** Develop targeted marketing campaigns and efficient sales funnels to reach your ideal customers and convert them into loyal patrons.
- **Embrace continuous improvement:** The market is dynamic, so be adaptable. Constantly analyze, iterate, and refine your processes and offerings to stay ahead of the curve.
- **The power of partnerships:** Collaborate with other hustlers in complementary niches to expand your reach and leverage each other's strengths.

The world awaits your disruption!

In the hustle world, time is your most valuable asset. By unleashing your inner drive, executing with laser focus, and launching your hustle empire at lightning speed, you position yourself for success and establish a competitive advantage that is difficult to replicate.

Hustlers Hackbook: A Masterclass on Navigating the Hustleverse

Remember, the competition waits for no one — so seize the moment, execute with precision, and let your hustle empire rise.

In our next master class, we'll explore "The Art of the Deal," where we'll delve into the strategies and tactics for effective communication, persuasion, and the ability to close deals with essential tools to secure clients, win negotiations, and dominate the competition. Until then, keep blitzing forward, and may your hustle empire conquer all. The world awaits your disruption!

THE ART OF THE DEAL

"Success in sales comes down to your ability to create a compelling narrative that inspires action." — *Chiemerie Sam Jonah*

Alright, hustlers, buckle up! Now, it's time to step into the heart of the hustle arena – the art of the deal. This is where empires are built, dreams are realized, and fortunes are won. But the arena is a battlefield, and success hinges on your ability to communicate effectively, persuade powerfully, and close deals like a champion.

This masterclass equips you with the ultimate weapon – your persuasive prowess. You'll learn to market yourself like a champion, negotiate like a gladiator, and master the psychology of influence. By the end of this class, you'll be closing deals left, right, and center, leaving your competitors weeping in the dust.

The Art of the Hustling Hustle

The hustle arena is a noisy battlefield. You need to make your voice heard, and you need to make it compelling. Let's face it, hustlers, some people are gifted salespeople, while others…well, not so much. But fear not! The hustling hustle is a learnable skill. We'll master the art of crafting persuasive messages, ethically influencing your audience, and leaving a lasting impression.

Hustlers Hackbook: A Masterclass on Navigating the Hustleverse

Think of it like this, Steve Jobs wasn't just a tech genius; he was a master marketer. His product launches were like rock concerts, creating excitement and anticipation that drove sales through the roof. You too can learn to captivate your audience, showcase the value you offer, and make them crave what you're selling. Steve Jobs wasn't just selling computers; he was selling a lifestyle, a revolution. Your hustle needs a story, a narrative that resonates with your ideal client and positions you as the ultimate solution to their problems.

Meet Zeniab, a pitch master who mesmerized investors with her charisma and conviction. Zeniab understood that successful pitches were not just about numbers and metrics but about storytelling — weaving a narrative that resonated with the audience's emotions and aspirations. By painting a vivid picture of the future, Zeniab secured the funding needed to turn her vision into reality.

In the hustle world, the ability to craft a compelling narrative can mean the difference between closing a deal and losing a prospect.

Here's how to craft your compelling Hustling narrative:

- **Know your audience:** Research your ideal client, understand their needs, pain points, and aspirations. Craft your message to speak directly to them.
- **The power of storytelling:** Facts tell, stories sell. Weave compelling narratives into your marketing materials, sales pitches, and client interactions.
- **Highlight your value proposition:** What makes you unique? Why should someone choose you over the competition? Clearly articulate your unique value proposition (UVP).

Negotiation Like a Champion

The hustle arena is a negotiation game. But forget about cutthroat tactics. Not all deals are created equal, hustlers. Negotiation is the art of finding common ground, creating win-win situations, and securing agreements that benefit you and your client. Remember this, Master negotiator Deepak Malhotra advises, "A good BATNA is your best defense against a bad deal." Your BATNA (Best Alternative To a Negotiated Agreement) is your walk-away option. Knowing your BATNA gives you leverage and ensures you don't get pressured into a bad deal.

Imagine you're negotiating a freelance contract. You want a higher rate, but the client has a tight budget. A skilled negotiator finds a compromise – perhaps a slightly lower rate in exchange for a longer-term contract or a referral bonus. Everyone walks away happy.

How to negotiate like a champ:

- **Do your research:** Know the market value of your services, competitor pricing, and industry standards.
- **Active listening:** Pay close attention to your client's needs and concerns.
- **Be prepared to walk away:** Don't be afraid to politely decline an offer that doesn't meet your needs. Your time and expertise are valuable.
- **Focus on value, not just price:** Highlight the long-term benefits your services will bring to the client, justifying your proposed rate.

The Psychology of Persuasion

The human mind is a fascinating thing, hustlers. And understanding the psychology of persuasion gives you a distinct edge in the hustled arena. People are persuaded by logic, yes, but also by emotions and subconscious cues. Unlocking the secrets of crafting persuasive arguments and ethically influencing your audience will get them to see things your way. Social psychologist Robert Cialdini identified six principles of persuasion: reciprocity, scarcity, authority, social proof, liking, and commitment. By understanding these principles, you can craft persuasive messages that resonate with your audience and gently nudge them towards the desired action.

Crafting Persuasive Arguments

- **Focus on benefits, not features:** Don't just list features of your product or service; explain how they will benefit the client's life or business.
- **Leverage social proof:** Showcase testimonials, case studies, and client success stories to build trust and credibility.
- **Use positive reinforcement:** Focus on the positive outcomes the client will achieve by working with you.
- **Create a sense of urgency:** Highlight limited-time offers or scarcity to encourage immediate action.

Reading the Room

Communication isn't just about words; it's about reading the room. It's also about what you hear (both verbally and nonverbally) and how you adapt your approach. Understanding nonverbal cues, like body language and facial expressions, allows you to tailor your approach and maximize the impact of your words. Imagine you're pitching your business idea to a potential investor. They're nodding along, making eye contact, and leaning in – positive signs that they're engaged. On the other hand, crossed arms, averted gazes, and fidgeting might indicate a lack of interest.

How to Read the Room:

- **Pay attention to body language:** Are they leaning in, engaged? Or are they crossed-armed, looking away? Adjust your approach accordingly.
- **Listen actively:** Don't just wait for your turn to speak. Listen attentively to the client's needs and concerns throughout the conversation.

- **Adapt your communication style:** Some clients prefer a direct approach, while others prefer a more consultative style. Be flexible and tailor your communication to their preferences.

Mastering the Art of the Deal

By mastering the art of the deal, you transform from a hustler into a deal-making maestro. **Adapt your communication style to match the other person's.** Are they analytical and data-driven? Back up your claims with facts and figures. Are they more emotional and relationship-oriented? Highlight the positive feelings and experiences your product or service will create.

Go and seal the deals!

By mastering the art of the deal, you transform from a hustler into a deal-making maestro. In the hustle arena, the art of the deal is your ultimate weapon. By mastering effective communication, persuasion, and negotiation techniques, you position yourself as a formidable contender who commands respect, wins clients, and dominates the competition. Remember, success in the hustle world is not just about what you know but also about how you communicate and connect with others.

In our next master class, we'll explore "The Money Game," where we'll delve into the Financial Strategies for Hustle Dominance. You'll gain financial literacy to manage cash flow effectively, avoid debt traps, and make sound financial decisions. Until then, keep sealing the deals!

THE MONEY GAME

"Financial freedom is available to those who learn about it and work for it." — Robert Kiyosaki

Hey Hustlers, let's face it: hustling isn't just about passion and drive – it's about building thriving businesses. And in the game of business, money talks. As we delve into the heart of the hustled world's engine – the money game – we'll equip you with the ultimate weapon: financial intelligence.

We'll transform you from a passionate hustler with a dream into a financially savvy powerhouse, armed with strategies to maximize income, outmaneuver competitors, and build a financial war chest to propel your long-term success. Remember, money is the fuel that propels your hustle empire and the key to managing cash flow, avoiding debt traps, and making sound decisions that propel your hustle forward.

Warren Buffet famously said, "Rule No. 1: Never lose money. Rule No. 2: Never forget rule No. 1." By managing your finances wisely, securing funding when needed, and making smart investments, you build a financial fortress that protects your hustle from unforeseen challenges and fuels your long-term growth.

Financial Fitness for Hustlers

Hustlers Hackbook: A Masterclass on Navigating the Hustleverse

Financial management isn't rocket science, but it's a crucial skill for any hustler. Understanding your financial fitness from the ground up, managing cash flow effectively, making sound investments, and avoiding pitfalls that can cripple your hustle before it takes off is the foundation for long-term hustle dominance.

Imagine a talented architect who lands a high-paying project. But instead of investing in his business – new software, marketing, or skill development – he blows it all on a luxury vacation. Soon, he's back to square one, struggling with cash flow and left with a mountain of debt. Financial fitness ensures you make smart financial decisions, re-investing profits back into your hustle for sustainable growth.

Meet David, a financial strategist who transformed struggling businesses into profitable enterprises. David's expertise wasn't just in numbers; it was in understanding the financial intricacies of the hustle world. By implementing smart budgeting, strategic pricing strategies, and prudent investment decisions, David helped his clients achieve financial stability and success.

In the hustle world, those who understand and master the principles of finance hold the keys to wealth and success.

How To Maintain Your Financial Fitness:

- **Cash Flow is King:** Understand the difference between revenue and profit. Focus on managing cash flow effectively to avoid cash flow gaps that could cripple your business. Utilize budgeting tools and accounting software to gain financial clarity.
- **Master the Art of Budgeting:** Create a clear budget to track income and expenses, identifying areas to optimize spending and maximize profitability.
- **Pay Yourself First:** Before you pay bills or indulge in luxuries, allocate a portion of your income towards savings and future investments to avoid lifestyle inflation.

- **Debt – Friend or Foe?:** Debt can be a powerful tool for growth, but it can also be a burden. Learn to utilize debt strategically and avoid getting trapped in a cycle of high-interest payments.
- **Embrace the Power of "No":** Don't be afraid to turn down projects that don't align with your financial goals or undervalue your expertise.

The Art of Pricing

The money game isn't just about making money; it's about making it smarter than your competitors. It's not just about how much you make, hustlers; it's about how much you keep. Here, you'll learn advanced financial strategies for pricing your services, managing costs, and crafting irresistible value propositions that leave clients reaching for their wallets.

Think of it like this: Richard Branson isn't just a successful entrepreneur; he's a master negotiator and value creator. He understands how to structure deals, price his products, and create irresistible value propositions that leave competitors wondering. You too can become a hustler who understands the financial intricacies of your industry and leverages them to your advantage.

Here's how to develop a strategic pricing model:

- **Pricing Strategies:** Explore different pricing models, from value-based pricing to tiered pricing, to find the sweet spot that maximizes revenue and customer satisfaction.
- **Cost Control is Key:** Identify and eliminate unnecessary expenses to optimize your bottom line. Every dollar saved is a dollar reinvested in your hustle's growth.
- **Competitive Analysis:** Understand your competitor's pricing strategy and value proposition. Find ways to differentiate yourself and offer greater value at a competitive price.

Hustlers Hackbook: A Masterclass on Navigating the Hustleverse

Building Your Financial War Chest

Building a thriving hustle empire takes resources. A financially secure hustler is a confident hustler. A strong financial war chest is the foundation of a thriving hustle empire. Understanding the strategies for securing funding, managing investments wisely, and building a strong financial war chest will fuel your long-term growth.

Mark Cuban, the billionaire investor, once said, "There's no shame in asking for money. It's a key part of the game." Learning how to secure funding, whether through personal savings, loans, or investor pitches, is crucial for scaling your hustle and achieving your full potential.

Meet Ike, an investor who strategically diversified his portfolio to mitigate risks and maximize returns. Ike understood the importance of building multiple income streams, from stocks and bonds to real estate and entrepreneurship. By spreading his investments across different asset classes, Ike safeguarded his financial future and positioned himself for long-term wealth accumulation.

Here's how to build financial war chest:

- **Bootstrapping Your Hustle:** Utilize your own resources, pre-sales, and creative financing options to launch and grow your business.
- **Exploring Funding Options:** Learn about different funding options like angel investors, venture capitalists, or crowdfunding platforms.
- **Investment Strategies:** Learn how to invest your profits wisely in assets that generate passive income or appreciate in value over time.
- **Build a Financial Safety Net:** Set aside emergency funds to cover unexpected expenses and protect your business from financial disruptions.
- **Building Wealth:** Develop a long-term financial plan that prioritizes wealth creation and financial security for yourself and

your family by harnessing the power of compound interest – the exponential growth of money over time through reinvesting earnings.

Keep winning the money game!

The Money Game isn't a spectator sport. By mastering the money game, you become more than just a hustler; you become a financial strategist. Equip yourself with financial knowledge, master strategic money moves, and build a financial war chest that fuels your long-term domination. So, go forth, manage your money wisely, and dominate the hustled world with both passion and financial prowess!

In our next master class, we'll explore "Brothers in Arms: Forging Strategic Alliances," where we'll delve into the art of building strategic partnerships – alliances that multiply your strength and influence. You'll gain an understanding of how to cultivate a network of informants, mentors, and collaborators to gain valuable intel and stay ahead of the curve. Until then, keep winning the money game!

BROTHERS IN ARMS

"If you want to go fast, go alone. If you want to go far, go together." — African Proverb

Alright, hustlers! Never forget this: Even the fiercest lone wolf needs backup sometimes. In the hustled world, strategic partnerships are the ultimate force multiplier. Understanding the art of building your strategic alliance network – a web of partnerships – will multiply your strength and influence, propelling you towards even greater dominance.

Forget the lone lion act; in the hustled world, collaboration is king. Now picture a pride of lions working together – they dominate the hunt. That's the power of strategic alliances. Learning how to identify potential allies, forge win-win partnerships, and cultivate a network of informants will keep you ahead of the curve. Remember, a rising tide lifts all boats, and by strategically aligning yourself with complementary forces, you create an unstoppable hustle powerhouse.

Building Your Strategic Alliance Network

Competition is fierce in the hustled world. But what if you could leverage the strengths of others to elevate your own hustle? Strategic partnerships are win-win collaborations where you combine forces with complementary businesses to create a more powerful offering. To build a strategic alliance network – a web of allies who share your vision but offer unique skills and resources – think about it like this: Imagine a freelance writer who partners with a web developer. The writer can craft compelling content, while the developer builds stunning websites.

Together, they offer a complete package to clients, increasing their value proposition and attracting more business than either could alone.

While both Uber and Spotify were powerhouses in their own right, their collaboration offering free Spotify subscriptions with Uber rides created a win-win situation for both companies – Uber attracted more riders, and Spotify gained new subscribers. Strategic partnerships can unlock incredible possibilities for all parties involved.

Meet Chinne and Ebube, two entrepreneurs who joined forces to conquer the competitive landscape. Chinne was a marketing maven with a flair for creativity, while Ebube was a finance whiz with a knack for numbers. By combining their talents and resources, they created a powerhouse partnership that outmaneuvered rivals and propelled their businesses to new heights.

In the hustle jungle, success belongs to those who recognize the value of collaboration and partnership.

How to Build Your Strategic Alliance Network:

- **Identify Potential Allies:** Look for brands with complementary offerings that don't directly compete with your hustle.
- **Clearly Defined Value Proposition:** Craft partnerships that offer clear benefits to both parties. What value can you offer your partner, and what value can they provide to you? For example, offer your expertise in exchange for access to their audience, resources, or distribution channels.
- **Structure the Alliance:** Define the terms of the partnership clearly, outlining roles, responsibilities, and profit-sharing agreements.
- **Formalize the Agreement:** Don't rely on handshakes. Create a clear agreement outlining expectations, responsibilities, and profit-sharing arrangements.

Negotiate Like a Kingpin

Hustlers Hackbook: A Masterclass on Navigating the Hustleverse

Building an alliance is just the first step. Negotiating a strategic alliance isn't about getting the better of your partner. It's about crafting a win-win situation that benefits both parties and lays the foundation for a long-term alliance. You need to be equipped with the skills to negotiate like a kingpin, crafting win-win partnerships that solidify your position in the hustled jungle.

Forget about one-sided victories. Negotiating a strategic alliance is about securing partnerships without conflict, maximizing the benefits for your hustle. Business magnate Jack Welch famously said, "A good deal is where everybody wins." Successful partnerships are built on trust, transparency, and a shared vision. Focus on creating a win-win scenario where both parties benefit from the collaboration.

How to Negotiate Effectively:

- **Do Your Due Diligence:** Research your potential partner's reputation, business model, target audience, and negotiating style to ensure a good fit.
- **Focus on Interests, Not Positions:** Don't get bogged down in arguing about details. Focus on the underlying needs and objectives of both parties, finding solutions that create value for everyone.
- **Ironclad Agreements:** Formalize your partnership with a clear contract outlining terms, roles, and responsibilities to avoid misunderstandings down the line.
- **Be Prepared to Walk Away:** Know your BATNA (Best Alternative To a Negotiated Agreement) and be willing to walk away if the partnership isn't mutually beneficial.

The Intel Advantage

Information is power, hustlers. And in the hustled world, the one with the best intel often reigns supreme. Strategic alliances aren't just about shared resources; they're about cultivating a network of informants – a web of informants, mentors, and collaborators who provide valuable insights and keep you one step ahead of the competition.

Imagine a group of street vendors with a network of sources – the taxi driver hears whispers of new trends, the flower seller knows about upcoming city events. By collaborating, they gain valuable intel that gives them a leg up on the competition. You can build your own intel advantage through strategic partnerships.

Think of it like this: a savvy investor doesn't rely solely on their own research. They consult analysts, financial advisors, and industry experts to gain a comprehensive understanding of the market. You too can build a network of advisors, mentors, and collaborators who share their knowledge and keep you informed of the latest trends and opportunities.

Former CIA Director, David Petraeus, famously said, "Good intelligence is critical to the success of any operation." By cultivating a network of trusted sources, you gain access to valuable intel, identify emerging trends, and anticipate potential challenges before they become roadblocks.

Meet Ruth, a master networker who leveraged her connections to gain valuable insights and opportunities. By nurturing relationships with industry insiders, thought leaders, and mentors, Ruth gained access to insider knowledge and strategic partnerships that propelled her hustle to new heights.

How To Develop Your Intel Network:

- **Develop Relationships with Key Players:** Network with industry leaders, influencers, and even competitors (sometimes!). Sharing information and fostering trust can lead to valuable intel exchanges.
- **Embrace Advisors:** Seek out advisors including journalists who can share their knowledge and experience, giving you valuable

insights into the industry landscape to stay abreast of the latest trends and developments.
- **Develop a Mentorship Relationship:** Find a seasoned hustler who can offer guidance, advice, and valuable connections.
- **Become an Information Hub:** Offer valuable insights and information to your network, fostering a spirit of reciprocity and increasing your value as a partner. Network with other hustlers, share best practices, and uncover valuable market insights.
- **Stay Connected:** Attend industry events, participate in online forums, and network with other hustlers to stay informed and build valuable connections.

Keep building your hustle cartel!

By forging strategic alliances, building a strategic alliance network, and cultivating a network of informants, you become a force to be reckoned with. You'll leverage the collective strengths of your allies, gain access to valuable intel, and navigate the hustled world with unparalleled foresight. Remember, hustlers, collaboration is key to long-term success. So, go forth, build your alliances, gather your intel, and conquer the hustled jungle with your pack by your side!

In our next master class, we'll explore "The Art of War: Strategies for Hustle Domination," where we'll delve into the advanced tactics and strategies for outmaneuvering your rivals and securing dominance. Until then, keep building your hustle cartel!

THE ART OF WAR

"The greatest victory is that which requires no battle." — *Sun Tzu*

The hustled world operates by its own rules. Here, mere survival isn't enough; you need to outmaneuver, outsmart, and outplay your competition to achieve true dominance. You need to be equipped with the battle-tested strategies used by hustle champions, from psychological warfare to harnessing the power of data-driven insights. Don't forget, hustlers, knowledge is power, and innovation is the key to staying ahead of the pack.

Psychological Warfare: Crippling Your Opponents

Competition is fierce, hustlers. Sometimes, winning comes down to outsmarting your rivals not just in tactics, but in mentality. In the hustled world, perception is reality. You need to understand the art of persuasion and mind games to exploit your opponents' weaknesses and gain a decisive edge. While I advocate for ethical business practices, understanding the psychology of competition is a valuable weapon.

Imagine you're a social media marketing agency competing for a major client. You discover your competitor is known for missed deadlines and poor client communication. By strategically highlighting your own strengths — reliability, responsiveness, and a focus on client satisfaction — you can plant seeds of doubt in the client's mind and position yourself as the superior choice.

Hustlers Hackbook: A Masterclass on Navigating the Hustleverse

Think of Muhammad Ali, the legendary boxer. He didn't just rely on brute strength; he used his trash-talking and mind games to demoralize his opponents before they even stepped into the ring. You too can master the art of psychological warfare, subtly influencing your competition's decisions and weakening their resolve.

Meet Uzo, a master persuader who utilized psychological tactics to sway clients and outmaneuver competitors. By understanding the psychological triggers that influence decision-making, Uzo was able to craft messages and strategies that resonated deeply with his audience, giving him a significant advantage in the marketplace.

In the hustle jungle, winning isn't just about brute force; it's about outsmarting your opponents without them even realizing it.

Codes for Psychological Warfare

- **Identify competitor weaknesses:** Research your rivals to uncover their areas of vulnerability, such as pricing models, customer service issues, or negative brand perception, and exploit them strategically.
- **The power of perception:** Shape how others perceive you and your competitors. Position yourself as the superior choice by highlighting your strengths and subtly exposing your competitor's weaknesses, but ensure your message remains ethical and grounded in facts.
- **Control the narrative:** Actively manage your brand reputation through strategic communication and proactive public relations to maintain a positive image in the face of potential competitor attacks.
- **The power of the counter-offensive:** Don't just react to your competitors' moves; anticipate them and launch strategic counter-attacks to disrupt their plans and keep them off-balance.
- **Confidence is key:** Project an aura of confidence and expertise. Belief in yourself is contagious. Act with confidence, and your

opponents will start questioning their own abilities. Nervousness breeds doubt in clients' minds, while confidence inspires trust and faith in your capabilities.

Information is Power: Outmaneuvering the Competition

Knowledge is a powerful weapon in the hustled world. Understanding the art of intelligence gathering, utilizing advanced research techniques will empower you to stay one step ahead of your competitors. Think of yourself as a cunning spy, gathering intel to anticipate your rivals' moves and exploit any vulnerabilities. Sun Tzu, the legendary Chinese military strategist, famously said, "Know yourself and know your enemy, and you will not be imperiled in a hundred battles." By understanding your competitor's strengths and weaknesses, market trends, and potential disruptions, you can preemptively adjust your strategies and seize opportunities before your rivals even see them coming.

Imagine a chess grandmaster preparing for their next match. They don't just memorize openings; they study their opponent's past games, identifying patterns and weaknesses. You too can become a hustler grandmaster, gathering intel, analyzing competitor strategies, and using this knowledge to predict their next moves and exploit any vulnerabilities.

How to gather information:

- **Competitor analysis:** Research your competitors' products, services, marketing strategies, and customer reviews to identify potential gaps in their offerings.
- **Embrace social listening:** Utilize social media monitoring tools to track industry conversations, understand customer sentiment towards your competitors, and identify potential opportunities.
- **Customer insights:** Conduct surveys and collect customer feedback to understand your target audience's needs, preferences, and potential pain points. Stay ahead of industry trends and

identify new customer needs through market research and competitor analysis.
- **Scenario planning:** Anticipate different scenarios and develop contingency plans so you're prepared for any move your competitor throws at you.
- **Embrace the element of surprise:** Don't let your rivals know your next move. Keep your strategies close to your chest and unleash them at the most opportune moment.

Data-Driven Warfare: The Ammunition of Champions

In today's hyper-competitive world, data is the ammunition that fuels victory. Data isn't just numbers on a spreadsheet; it's a weapon wielded most effectively by those who hold the key to victory. Understanding the power of data analytics and market intelligence to outsmart your rivals and make strategic decisions based on hard facts, not gut feelings, is crucial. Business magnate Jeff Bezos famously said, "In data we trust." Jeff Bezos doesn't rely on gut instincts to run Amazon; he leverages sophisticated data analysis tools to understand customer behavior and personalize their shopping experience. Data empowers you to make informed decisions, identify market opportunities, and stay ahead of the curve. By analyzing user data, market trends, and competitor performance, you gain invaluable insights that inform your strategies, optimize your marketing campaigns, and give you a decisive edge in the marketplace.

Meet Jecinta, a data maverick who revolutionized her industry by leveraging advanced analytics to uncover hidden trends and opportunities. By harnessing the power of data, Jecinta was able to make strategic investments, optimize operations, and outmaneuver competitors with precision and agility.

How To Fortify Your Hustle With Data:

- **Track your data:** Invest in analytics tools to track website traffic, social media engagement, and customer behavior to gain insights into your audience and their preferences.
- **A/B testing is your friend:** Experiment with different marketing messages, website layouts, and pricing strategies using A/B testing to identify the most effective options.
- **Identify key metrics:** Focus on metrics that matter — customer acquisition costs, customer lifetime value, and conversion rates. Track these metrics and use them to optimize your performance.
- **Data-driven decision making:** Don't rely on gut instinct; base your decisions on real-world data and actionable insights gleaned from your analytics.
- **Embrace automation:** Utilize data automation tools to analyze vast amounts of data and gain actionable insights efficiently.

Innovate or Die: Staying Ahead of the Pack

The hustled world is a constant state of change. What works today might be obsolete tomorrow. That's why innovation is the lifeblood of success and the hustled world rewards those who embrace it. Understanding the importance of fostering a culture of innovation and developing disruptive tools and strategies will help you to stay ahead of the curve and lead the charge in shaping your industry's future.

Think of it like this, Steve Jobs didn't just sell computers; he revolutionized the way we interact with technology. Don't be afraid to challenge the status quo and develop groundbreaking products or services that disrupt the market and redefine customer expectations.

Remember, hustlers, the only way to remain dominant is to constantly evolve and adapt.

How to stay ahead through Innovation:

- **Embrace a growth mindset:** Cultivate a culture that encourages experimentation, risk-taking, and a constant pursuit of improvement.
- **Invest in R&D:** Allocate resources for research and development to stay ahead of technological advancements and develop innovative solutions to emerging customer needs.
- **Embrace design thinking:** By putting yourself in the shoes of your customers, empathizing with their needs and desires, and iterating on solutions based on feedback, you can develop products and services that resonate deeply and drive success in the marketplace.

Keep dominating your territory!

In the hustle jungle, victory belongs to those who master the art of war — the strategic deployment of psychological tactics, information intelligence, data analytics, and innovation. By honing these advanced strategies, you position yourself as a formidable contender who dominates the competition and shapes the future of your industry.

In our next master class, we'll explore "Respect the Hustle Code," where we'll delve into the language, ethics, and legal landscape of the hustle arena. You'll gain the legal knowledge to protect your hustle, avoid common pitfalls, and operate within the boundaries of the law. Until then, keep dominating your territory!

RESPECT THE GAME

"It takes 20 years to build a reputation and five minutes to ruin it. If you think about that, you'll do things differently." — *Warren Buffett*

Alright, hustlers! Take note: Even the most ferocious lion needs to understand the rules of the jungle. The hustled world isn't a lawless wasteland; there's a code of honor among hustlers. The hustle arena has its own etiquette, laws, and language. As we delve deep into the Hustle Code – the unspoken rules, ethics, and legalities that govern this fast-paced world – you will master this code because it is crucial for navigating its complexities and emerging not just victorious, but respected.

The Code of the Arena: Hustling with Honor

Hustlers thrive on competition, but even gladiators have a code of honor. Hustlers, let's get this straight – cutting corners and burning bridges won't win you the game. As we explore the importance of ethical hustling, we'll learn how to maintain a positive reputation, build trust with clients, and foster a network of allies who respect your hustle and want to collaborate with you – these are the cornerstones of long-term success in the hustle jungle.

Imagine you're a web developer approached by two potential clients. Client A offers a higher fee but wants you to copy a competitor's design, essentially stealing their intellectual property. Client B offers a fair price and wants you to create an original design. The choice is clear – building a reputation for ethical practices attracts better clients, fosters trust, and fuels long-term growth. Hustling with honor attracts allies and fuels long-term success. Business magnate Warren Buffet famously said, "It takes 20 years to build a reputation and five minutes to ruin it. If you think about that, you'll do things differently." Hustling with honor builds a strong reputation that attracts loyal clients, trustworthy partners, and fuels sustainable success.

Meet Usman, an ethical hustler who prioritized honesty and integrity in all his dealings. Despite the cutthroat nature of the hustle world, Usman's reputation for fair play and integrity earned him the respect and trust of clients, collaborators, and competitors alike, ultimately paving the way for long-term success and prosperity. In an environment where trust is currency, maintaining integrity and ethical conduct is essential for building a solid foundation of success.

How to Hustle With Honour:

- Stand by your values: Define your core values and principles. Don't compromise your integrity for short-term gains. Build your hustle on a foundation of integrity.
- Underpromise, overdeliver: Set realistic expectations with clients and consistently exceed them. This builds trust and loyalty, making them more likely to return for future projects and recommend you to others.
- Treat everyone with respect: From clients to competitors, treat everyone with courtesy and professionalism. You never know who might become a valuable ally down the line. A good reputation attracts more opportunities than negativity ever will.
- Give back to the community: Share your knowledge, mentor aspiring hustlers, and contribute to the growth of your industry. This goodwill fosters a sense of camaraderie and positions you as a leader, not just a competitor.

The Fine Line: Ethics vs. Aggressive Tactics

Hustlers Hackbook: A Masterclass on Navigating the Hustleverse

The hustled world demands a certain level of aggressiveness – after all, competition is fierce. But there's a fine line between aggressive tactics and unethical conduct. Understanding the tools to navigate that line will ensure your hustle is effective while maintaining a shred of decency. Think of it like this, Michael Jordan was a fierce competitor, pushing himself and his teammates to excel. However, he earned respect because of his dedication and sportsmanship. Hustling hard is admirable, but playing dirty will only tarnish your reputation and damage your long-term prospects.

How to Hustle Ethically:

- Know your boundaries: Clearly define your personal and professional ethics – your ethical red lines – and never cross them. What tactics are off-limits for you, regardless of the potential gain?
- Transparency is key: Be upfront and honest with your clients in your dealings. Hidden fees, misleading claims, and manipulative tactics will backfire in the long run. Exploitation, manipulation, or deceptive practices have no place in sustainable hustle.
- Seek external perspectives: Bounce ideas off trusted advisors or mentors to get a reality check on the ethical implications of your chosen strategies.

Legal Maneuvers: Protecting Your Hustle Empire

The hustled world has its own legal landscape, its own set of legal boundaries, and ignoring the law can bring your empire crashing down. When you are equipped with basic legal knowledge to protect your hustle from lawsuits, you will understand how to avoid common pitfalls, operate within your rights and obligations, and know when to seek professional legal counsel. Legal expert Harvey Specter famously said, "The only thing more dangerous than your enemies are your blind spots." Ignorance of the law is no excuse. Familiarize yourself with intellectual property rights, contract law, and any industry-specific regulations to avoid costly legal battles and protect your hustle from unforeseen challenges.

A savvy entrepreneur wouldn't build a house on shaky foundations. By understanding basic legal principles like intellectual property rights, contract law, and data privacy regulations, you build a solid foundation for your hustle and minimize your risk of legal trouble.

Meet Osas, a legal eagle who leveraged her expertise to protect her hustle empire. By understanding the legal landscape, Osas preemptively addressed potential risks and liabilities, drafted airtight contracts, and navigated legal disputes with confidence and clarity, ensuring the longevity and success of her hustle ventures.

How To Protect Your Hustle Legally:

- Invest in basic legal education: Take online courses or attend workshops to gain a foundational understanding of business law, intellectual property rights, and contract basics.
- Consult with a legal professional: Seek advice from a qualified lawyer to understand your legal obligations, draft sound contracts, and protect your intellectual property.
- Stay informed: Keep up with changes in relevant laws and regulations to ensure your hustle operates within the legal framework. Many industry associations and government websites offer free resources.
- Prioritize ethical conduct: Playing by the rules not only protects you legally but also fosters trust and builds a sustainable business.

Keep respecting the code of the arena!

In the hustle jungle, respect for the game is paramount. By understanding and adhering to the principles of the hustle code — maintaining integrity, navigating ethical grey areas, and operating within the boundaries of the law — you build a solid foundation of trust, reputation, and success that propels you towards victory in the competitive landscape.

In our next master class, we'll explore "Beyond the Money," where we'll explore the diverse rewards that come from the hustle journey. You'll discover how hustling empowers you to take control of your career path, work on your own terms, and achieve the freedom to pursue your passions. Explore the concept of leaving a lasting impact through your hustle, from shaping your industry to inspiring future generations. And embrace the inherent satisfaction that comes from overcoming challenges, achieving goals, and constantly pushing yourself to new heights. Until then, keep respecting the code of the arena!

BEYOND THE MONEY

'Financial freedom is a sweet reward, but the benefits extend far beyond that' - *Chiemerie Sam Jonah*

Alright, hustlers! We've secured the fat stacks – the financial rewards of a thriving hustle. But there's more to this game than just cold, hard cash. Understanding the rich harvest of intangible rewards that come from hustling hard and smart are the rewards that fuel your soul, push you further, and make the journey itself just as rewarding as the destination. Sure, financial freedom is a sweet reward, but the hustle dividend extends far beyond that. We're talking about control, legacy, and the thrill of the climb. These are the dividends that keep you pushing forward, even when the going gets tough.

Freedom & Autonomy

Hustling isn't just about chasing money; it's about chasing freedom. The corporate grind isn't for everyone. Some are stuck in dead-end jobs, yearning for the flexibility to pursue their passions. The hustle empowers you to break free from the constraints of traditional employment, becoming your own boss, charting your own course, and working on your own terms. This freedom allows you to pursue your passions, design your own work schedule, pursue ventures that truly excite you, and create a work-life balance that fuels your well-being and fuels your hustle. Picture a talented graphic designer who leaves their soul-sucking agency job to start their own freelance business. They now have the freedom to choose their clients, work on projects they're passionate about, and achieve a work-life balance that allows them to pursue their hobbies. This is the power of the hustle – designing your dream life, not someone else's.

Nelson Mandela famously said, "For to be free is not merely to cast off one's chains, but to live in a way that respects and enhances the freedom of others." Hustling grants you the freedom to pursue your passions, but it also comes with the responsibility to use that freedom to create a positive impact on the world around you.

Meet Kosi, a corporate employee who felt trapped in her 9-to-5 job, longing for the freedom to pursue her creative passions. Through hustling on the side, Kosi gradually built a successful freelance business, allowing her to quit her job and embrace a lifestyle of autonomy and fulfillment. By taking control of her career path, Kosi found a newfound sense of purpose and freedom that transformed her life.

In the hustle jungle, finding work that aligns with your passions and values is not just a luxury; it's a strategic imperative for long-term success and fulfillment.

How to Find Your Freedom:

- Define your ideal work-life balance: What does freedom look like for you? Do you crave flexibility, location independence, or simply more time for your loved ones?
- Develop a long-term hustle vision: Craft a clear vision for your ideal career path, one that aligns with your passions and allows you to achieve your desired level of freedom.
- Embrace continuous learning: The hustle landscape constantly evolves. Invest in your education and skill development to maintain your competitive edge and expand your freedom to pursue new opportunities.

Building Your Legacy

Hustlers Hackbook: A Masterclass on Navigating the Hustleverse

The hustle isn't just about building an empire; it's about leaving a lasting impact. You can shape your industry, inspire future generations, and contribute to a cause you care about. This sense of purpose adds a deeper meaning to your hustle and fuels your desire to achieve greatness. Imagine a visionary entrepreneur who develops an innovative product that disrupts an entire industry, improves countless lives, and inspires countless others to pursue their own entrepreneurial dreams. This entrepreneur's legacy is far greater than just financial success; they've created a positive ripple effect that impacts generations to come. This is the power of building a legacy – leaving a positive footprint on the world through your hustle. Maya Angelou famously said, "Success is not about how much you have in life, but about what you do with what you have." Your hustle legacy isn't just about financial gain; it's about the positive change you create, the problems you solve, and the inspiration you provide to others. Hustle with purpose, with a vision to create something that will stand the test of time and inspire others to chase their dreams.

How To Build Your Hustle Legacy:

- **Identify your cause:** What issues or challenges are you passionate about solving? Aligning your hustle with a cause creates a deeper sense of purpose and legacy.
- **Give back to your community:** Use your success to mentor aspiring hustlers, support charitable causes, or contribute to the betterment of your industry.
- **Mentor and inspire others:** Share your hustle story, your knowledge and experience with aspiring hustlers to inspire and empower others to chase their dreams and achieve their own success stories.

The Thrill of the Climb

Hustlers Hackbook: A Masterclass on Navigating the Hustleverse

The hustle isn't always sunshine and roses, hustlers. But let's be honest — there's an intrinsic satisfaction that comes from overcoming challenges, achieving goals, and constantly pushing yourself to new heights. The thrill of the climb is a powerful motivator, fueling your hustle journey and keeping you engaged in the pursuit of excellence.

Imagine a young entrepreneur facing countless setbacks but persevering through sheer grit and determination. Finally, their innovative product gains traction and disrupts the market. The sense of accomplishment, the thrill of victory, and the knowledge they beat the odds — these are the intrinsic rewards that make the hustle so addictive.

Nelson Mandela also said, "After climbing a great hill, no one finds out how many times one stumbled." The hustle journey is paved with challenges, but the thrill of overcoming them and the satisfaction of reaching new heights is a reward all its own. It always seems impossible until it's done, so embrace the challenges of the hustle journey. The grit, perseverance, and determination you develop along the way are just as rewarding as the final victory.

How to Get Satisfaction from Your Hustle:

- Set audacious goals: Don't settle for mediocrity. Push yourself beyond your comfort zone and set ambitious goals that excite and motivate you.
- Celebrate your wins (big and small): Acknowledge your achievements, no matter how seemingly insignificant. This reinforces positive behaviors and keeps you motivated.
- Embrace a growth mindset: View challenges as opportunities to learn and grow. Setbacks are stepping stones to future success. Every obstacle overcome strengthens your hustle muscle.
- Find your hustle flow: Immerse yourself in the process of hustling, the act of creation, and the pursuit of your vision.

Hustlers Hackbook: A Masterclass on Navigating the Hustleverse

Enjoy the rewards of the hustle!

In the hustle jungle, the rewards go far beyond just financial gains. From freedom and autonomy to building a legacy and embracing the thrill of the climb, hustling offers a rich tapestry of rewards that enrich your life in countless ways. By embracing these diverse dividends of hustle, you can create a life of purpose, passion, and lasting impact.

In our next master class, we'll explore "The Evolving Hustle," where we'll explore potential future challenges and strategies for adapting your hustle to thrive in a changing world. We'll delve into strategies for staying up-to-date on industry trends, identifying emerging technologies that might impact your hustle, and adapting your approach to leverage new opportunities. Until then, enjoy the rewards of the hustle!

Hustlers Hackbook: A Masterclass on Navigating the Hustleverse

THE EVOLVING HUSTLE

"The only constant is change." - Heraclitus

Alright, hustlers! Listen up – the hustled world is a living beast, constantly evolving and adapting. The strategies that brought you here might not guarantee future dominance. Understanding potential disruptions, emerging challenges, and equipping yourself with strategies to adapt and thrive in a world constantly reshaping itself is paramount. As we delve into the concept of the ever-evolving hustle, we will emphasize the importance of continuous learning and adaptation to ensure your hustle remains relevant and dominant.

Remember, hustlers, the only certainty is change. The hustle landscape you navigate today might be unrecognizable tomorrow. The key to future success lies in your ability to anticipate change, embrace disruption, and navigate the learning curve to future-proof your hustle, keeping you on top.

The Rise of Automation

The march of technology is relentless, a double-edged sword. While it fuels innovation, it can also disrupt industries. The rise of automation and artificial intelligence (AI) is a force to be reckoned with. Understanding the potential impact of automation and artificial intelligence (AI) on your hustle equips you with strategies to leverage these technologies to your advantage.

Imagine a freelance writer facing a future where AI can generate human-quality content at lightning speed. Our writer, resistant to change, sticks to traditional methods and gets left behind. But a savvy competitor embraces AI writing tools, utilizes them to generate draft content, and then focuses on the creative aspects that AI can't replicate – like crafting compelling narratives and injecting a human touch. This competitor thrives in the face of automation.

Elon Musk, a visionary entrepreneur, famously said, "The future of artificial intelligence is very scary. It's capable of surpassing human capabilities." While AI might automate certain tasks, it won't replace human ingenuity and creativity. The hustlers who leverage AI to their advantage, not fear it, will conquer the future.

Meet Oluebube, a hustler in the transportation industry who embraced the rise of automation. As intelligent transport systems began to revolutionize the transportation sector, Oluebube recognized the potential for disruption in his business. Instead of resisting change, he invested in learning about autonomous vehicle technology, automated fleet management systems retrained his workforce, and adapted his business model to incorporate automation. By leveraging technology rather than fearing it, Oluebube not only is surviving disruption but also positioned himself as a leader in the automated transportation market.

In the hustle jungle, those who anticipate future trends and adapt their strategies accordingly will be best positioned to thrive in a changing world.

How to Leverage Automation:

- **Identify automatable tasks in your hustle:** Analyze your workflow and learn how to integrate AI tools seamlessly into your hustle workflow to maximize efficiency and productivity.
- **Upskill in complementary areas:** Focus on developing skills that complement AI, such as critical thinking, problem-solving, creativity, and emotional intelligence – areas where humans will always hold the edge.
- **Embrace lifelong learning:** Stay ahead of the curve by continuously learning new skills and staying informed about advancements in automation and AI.

The Evolving Hustle Landscape

The future hustled world might be radically different from what we know today. This chapter encourages you to anticipate potential disruptions – economic shifts, social changes, even technological breakthroughs – and develop contingency plans to navigate unknown challenges.

Imagine a savvy entrepreneur who anticipates a major shift in consumer preferences towards ethical and sustainable business practices. They adapt their business model to cater to this evolving market, ensuring their long-term success. This is future-proofing your hustle on a grand scale – anticipating major disruptions and proactively adapting to remain relevant.

Charles Darwin, the father of evolution, famously said, "It is not the strongest of the species that survives, nor the most intelligent that survives. It is the one that is most adaptable to change." Don't be afraid to reinvent yourself. Embrace a flexible mindset, stay informed about potential disruptions, and be prepared to adapt your hustle to conquer the uncharted territories of the future.

How to Future-Proof Your Hustle:

- Develop future scenarios: Brainstorm potential future disruptions that might impact your industry and explore various ways your hustle could adapt to each scenario.
- Cultivate a network of forward-thinkers: Connect with individuals who are passionate about the future and can provide valuable insights into emerging trends and potential disruptions.
- Maintain a learning agility: Stay curious, embrace continuous learning, and be prepared to acquire new skills to navigate the evolving landscape of the future hustle.

Embrace the Learning Curve

The hustled world rewards lifelong learners. Complacency is the enemy of the hustle. True champions understand that learning is a lifelong journey. The message is clear – never stop learning, growing, and pushing your boundaries.

Understanding the importance of cultivating a growth mindset, constantly seeking out new challenges, and developing new skills equips you to stay relevant and dominant. Imagine a marketing guru clinging to outdated marketing tactics in the face of the digital revolution. They refuse to learn new skills like social media marketing or content creation. Their once-dominant strategies become obsolete, and their hustle suffers. This is the danger of complacency – the hustled world doesn't wait for anyone.

Albert Einstein, a brilliant physicist, famously said, "The important thing is not to stop questioning. Curiosity has its own reason for existing." Curiosity and a relentless pursuit of knowledge are your weapons against a constantly evolving hustle landscape. Embrace challenges as opportunities to learn, develop new skillsets, and stay relevant in the face of change.

Meet Emily, a hustler who recognized the importance of continuous learning in staying ahead of the curve. Despite her initial success in the fashion industry, Emily understood that complacency was the enemy of progress. She enrolled in online courses, attended industry conferences, and sought out mentors to expand her skill set and stay abreast of emerging trends. Through her dedication to learning and adaptation, Emily not only maintained her competitive edge but also positioned herself as a leader in her field.

"The illiterate of the 21st century will not be those who cannot read and write, but those who cannot learn, unlearn, and relearn." — Alvin Toffler

In the hustleverse, those who are willing to embrace the learning process and adapt to new challenges will thrive, while those who resist change risk being left behind.

Technique for Growth:

- **Develop a growth mindset:** Challenge the fixed mindset of "I can't" and adopt the growth mindset of "I can learn." Embrace challenges as opportunities to learn and grow.
- **Seek out continuous learning:** Read industry publications, attend workshops and conferences, or take online courses to stay updated on the latest trends and technologies.
- **Develop a learning routine**: Dedicate time each week to learning new skills, attending workshops, or reading industry publications.
- **Seek out mentors:** Connect with experienced hustlers in your industry. Learn from their successes and failures, and gain valuable insights to inform your own hustle journey.
- **Embrace online courses:** The internet is a treasure trove of knowledge. Invest in online courses to acquire new skills, hone your existing expertise, and stay ahead of the curve.
- **Embrace new challenges:** Don't be afraid to experiment with new strategies, explore uncharted territory, and develop new skillsets to enhance your hustle arsenal.

Keep learning, adapt your hustle, and continue to conquer the world!

The future of hustle is a thrilling unknown. The ever-evolving hustle rewards those who are nimble, adaptable, and constantly learning. By embracing the growth mindset, future-proofing your hustle, preparing for disruption, and possessing the agility to adapt, you'll ensure your hustle continues to thrive in the face of change. Remember, the future belongs to those who can navigate the unknown and emerge victorious. So, go forth, keep learning, adapt your hustle, and continue to conquer the world!

In our final chapter, "The Enduring Hustle," we'll reflect on the journey thus far, celebrate the resilience we've cultivated, and chart the course for continued success in the hustle jungle. Until then, embrace the learning

Hustlers Hackbook: A Masterclass on Navigating the Hustleverse

THE ETERNAL HUSTLER:

A LIFELONG JOURNEY

Alright, hustlers! We've reached the conclusion of this masterclass. You've conquered challenges, devoured knowledge, and emerged as a master of the hustled world. But remember, the arena isn't just a battleground – it's a classroom, a testing ground, and a breeding ground for innovation.

This closing note celebrates the spirit of the eternal hustler. It's a call to embrace the lifelong journey of the hustle, a journey paved with lessons learned, relentless pursuit, and an unwavering commitment to excellence.

The Arena: Lessons Learned

Take a moment to reflect. The hustle arena is a crucible. It throws fire at you, tests your limits, and demands constant evolution. Consider further the invaluable lessons you've learned:

Workbook:

- Grab your workbook and revisit the exercises from each chapter. Reflect on your progress, identify areas for further growth, and set new goals to propel your hustle forward.

Hustlers Hackbook: A Masterclass on Navigating the Hustleverse

- Jot down your key takeaways from this journey. What did you learn about yourself as a hustler? What strategies resonated with you the most?
- Document your success stories. Capture the challenges you overcame, the strategies you employed, and the lessons learned from each victory.

This workbook, your personal hustle companion, is now filled with your insights, experiences, and the unique roadmap you've charted for your hustle journey. The lessons learned in the arena are your weapons – tools to overcome obstacles, seize opportunities, and build your hustle empire..

The Relentless Pursuit

Remember, hustlers, the hustle is a lifelong journey, not a destination. There will be setbacks, there will be roadblocks, but there will also be triumphs and moments of pure hustler glory. Embrace the challenges as opportunities to learn and adapt. Celebrate the victories as milestones on your journey. Never stop learning, growing, and evolving as a hustler.

Mahatma Gandhi, the iconic leader of India's independence movement, famously said, "Be the change that you wish to see in the world." The hustle is not just about personal gain; it's about making an impact, leaving your mark, and changing the game for the better.

Challenges are inevitable, but they are also opportunities for growth. Learn from your setbacks, celebrate your victories, and never lose the insatiable curiosity and drive that fuels your hustle.

The Eternal Flame

Hustlers, your worth isn't defined by your wins or losses. It's defined by the fire that burns within – the relentless pursuit of excellence, the unwavering commitment to growth, and the audacious spirit that propels you forward. Now go forth, conquer the arena, and leave your mark on the world, one hustle at a time! Remember, the hustleverse needs your relentless spirit, your innovative ideas, and your unwavering determination. Go forth and be the change, the leader, the eternal hustler this world needs.

Now go forth, hustlers! Take the lessons learned, the strategies mastered, and the hustler's manifesto etched in your heart. Conquer the arena, chase your dreams with relentless passion, and leave your mark on the world. Remember, the hustle never ends, but the rewards are limitless.

The Hustler's Manifesto

And so, I leave you with the words of the eternal hustler's manifesto:

"I am a hustler, relentless in my pursuit of greatness. I embrace challenges as opportunities for growth. I celebrate victories with humility and gratitude. I am defined not by my wins or losses but by my unwavering commitment to excellence. I am the eternal flame that burns bright in the hustle arena. I am a hustler, and the world is my playground."

The hustle never stops! But you don't have to go it alone.

- Want to connect with a community of like-minded hustlers? Join my private Telegram Channel, "The Hustlenaires." Share your struggles, celebrate your victories, and get inspired by the journeys of others.
- Ready to take your hustle to the next level? Book a free 30-minute consultation call with me to discuss your specific goals and develop a personalized hustle plan.

Thank you for joining me on this exploration of the hustleverse. You've learned valuable strategies, conquered challenges, and discovered the fire that burns within you – the relentless spirit of the eternal hustler. Now, go forth and chase your dreams with unwavering passion! Remember, the world needs your unique hustle, your innovative ideas, and your relentless determination. Go out there and make your mark!

This concludes the masterclass, but the hustle journey continues. Keep hustling, keep learning, and keep conquering. Until next time!

ABOUT THE AUTHOR

Chiemerie Samuel Jonah is a highly sought-after socioeconomic projects management consultant, a systems strategist, logistics expert and a development entrepreneur. He is the Founder/CEO of Induvas Group, the mother company of four subsidiaries; and the President of Induvas Commonwealth Network-a fast-growing network of Independent Consultants. He is equally the MD of Obarn Trading and Logistics Ltd., a leading provider of integrated logistics and supply chain management solutions.

Chiemerie has a proven track record of driving successful multi-billion Naira projects and implementing strategic initiatives. He is committed to enhancing economic viability and empowering individuals and communities through socioeconomic impact projects.

His passion lies in empowering individuals and communities to reach their full potential by harnessing the transformative power of value creation. Chiemerie is more than just a business leader; I'm a beacon of wealth creation, demonstrating that true prosperity goes beyond material riches. It's about the enduring legacy of value we create in the world.